EXPLORING COUNTRIES

France

by Rachel Grack

BLASTOFF! READERS 5

Note to Librarians, Teachers, and Parents:

Blastoff! Readers are carefully developed by literacy experts and combine standards-based content with developmentally appropriate text.

Level 1 provides the most support through repetition of high-frequency words, light text, predictable sentence patterns, and strong visual support.

Level 2 offers early readers a bit more challenge through varied simple sentences, increased text load, and less repetition of high-frequency words.

Level 3 advances early-fluent readers toward fluency through increased text and concept load, less reliance on visuals, longer sentences, and more literary language.

Level 4 builds reading stamina by providing more text per page, increased use of punctuation, greater variation in sentence patterns, and increasingly challenging vocabulary.

Level 5 encourages children to move from "learning to read" to "reading to learn" by providing even more text, varied writing styles, and less familiar topics.

Whichever book is right for your reader, Blastoff! Readers are the perfect books to build confidence and encourage a love of reading that will last a lifetime!

This edition first published in 2012 by Bellwether Media, Inc.

No part of this publication may be reproduced in whole or in part without written permission of the publisher. For information regarding permission, write to Bellwether Media, Inc., Attention: Permissions Department, 5357 Penn Avenue South, Minneapolis, MN 55419.

Library of Congress Cataloging-in-Publication Data

Koestler-Grack, Rachel A., 1973-
France / by Rachel Grack.
    p. cm. – (Blastoff! readers: Exploring countries)
Includes bibliographical references and index.
Summary: "Developed by literacy experts for students in grades three through seven, this book introduces young readers to the geography and culture of France"–Provided by publisher.
ISBN 978-1-60014-671-8 (paperback : alk. paper)
1. France–Juvenile literature. 2. France–Social life and customs–Juvenile literature. I. Title.
DC33.K64 2010   944–dc22   2010009214

Text copyright © 2012 by Bellwether Media, Inc. BLASTOFF! READERS and associated logos are trademarks and/or registered trademarks of Bellwether Media, Inc.
Printed in the United States of America, North Mankato, MN.   080111   1191

Contents

Did you know?

France also includes the overseas regions of French Guiana in South America, Réunion in the Indian Ocean, and Guadeloupe and Martinique in the Caribbean.

Atlantic Ocean

fun fact

Because France has six sides, French people often call their country "the hexagon."

France covers an area of 248,429 square miles (643,427 square kilometers), making it the largest country in western Europe. France shares borders with Belgium, Luxembourg, Germany, Switzerland, Italy, Monaco, Andorra, and Spain. The capital of France is Paris.

Three bodies of water touch France. The English Channel runs between France and Great Britain. West of France is the Bay of Biscay and, beyond it, the Atlantic Ocean. The Mediterranean Sea beats against France's rocky southern shores.

Did you know?

The Seine is a major river in France. It starts in eastern France, flows through Paris, and empties into the English Channel.

France is made up of many different landscapes. There are rivers, lakes, marshes, mountains, and **plateaus**. Flat plains and low, rolling hills stretch across most of France. The Paris **Basin**, France's most famous **lowland**, covers about 54,000 square miles (140,000 square kilometers) of the area around Paris. France is well known for its scenic coasts. The Mediterranean coastline is often called the French Riviera.

Mont Blanc

fun fact

Mont Blanc is about 15,770 feet (4,807 meters) tall. Its height changes from year to year based on the amount of snow on its peak.

France boasts five major mountain ranges. The French Alps stretch along the border between France and Italy. These mountains include Mont Blanc, the highest peak in western Europe. The Jura Mountains lie north of the Alps, and the Vosges Mountains run along the border between France and Germany. France and Spain are divided by the rugged Pyrenees, and the forest-covered Ardennes spill into Belgium and Luxembourg.

The Massif Central covers about one-sixth of France. It is the largest plateau in the country. The Auvergne Mountains are part of the Massif Central. Over the last 70,000 years, volcanic eruptions have created and shaped these mountains. The last eruption occurred about 7,000 years ago.

Along with rounded mountain peaks, the Massif Central has deep river **gorges**. The Massif Central's rugged terrain makes the climate there less mild than in other areas of France. Summers are cooler, and winters often bring cold temperatures and heavy snowfalls.

fun fact

The Massif Central is the largest area of extinct volcanoes in the world. About 450 inactive volcanoes lie in the Massif Central.

Pont d'Arc

Did you know?

People often kayak or canoe through the river gorges of the Massif Central. Along the way, they take in views like the Pont d'Arc and other natural land features.

lynx

wolf

Did you know?

By the 1930s, wolves were extinct in France. Recently, wolves have come back to France from Italy through the Alps.

dolphin

The wildlife of France is as varied as the landscape. A type of wild goat called the chamois lives in the mountains of France. Chamois are excellent climbers and have been spotted near the top of Mont Blanc. Brown bears, lynx, and leopard-spotted genets also live in the mountains.

fun fact

Camargue foals are born with brown or black fur. Their fur turns white as they grow.

The forests of France are home to deer, foxes, hares, badgers, and wild boars. Herds of wild Camargue horses wander the marshes and wetlands of southern France. Snakes and lizards can also be found in parts of the country. Off the coasts of France, dolphins are often seen jumping in the water or swimming beside boats.

About 64 million people call France home. The French come from the Roman, West German, Norman, and Celtic peoples. Each group's **ancestors** settled in a different area of France. They established their own customs and languages. Over time, the French language developed.

The **Basque people** live in the Pyrenees. They speak their own distinct language, called Euskera. However, most groups speak French, the country's official language.

Speak French!

English	French	How to say it
hello	bonjour	bohn- JOOR
good-bye	au revoir	oh ruh-VWAHR
yes	oui	WHEE
no	non	NOH
please	s'il vous plaît	SEEL VOO PLAY
thank you	merci	mayr-SEE
friend (male)	ami	ah-MEE
friend (female)	amie	ah-MEE

fun fact

Around 4.5 million people ride the Paris Metro every day.

Most people in France live in cities. They do a lot of walking, but they also use buses and the subway to get around. They shop at small neighborhood stores. Each shop specializes in one type of product. For example, the *boulangerie* sells breads and pastries. People buy meat at the *boucherie*, or the butcher's shop. French people usually buy bread, meat, and milk fresh each day.

Some French people live in the countryside. Small farms dot the landscapes around villages and towns. People use cars and trains to go from place to place. Children who live on farms help their parents with daily chores. They feed animals, gather eggs, and milk cows. Some children help plant and pick crops.

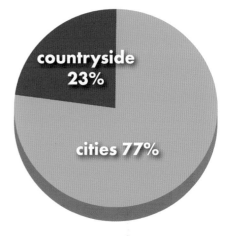

Where People Live in France

countryside 23%

cities 77%

In France, children are required to go to school until they are 15 years old. By age 4, most French children are in *école maternelle*, or nursery school. From ages 6 to 11, children attend *école élémentaire*, or elementary school. Their classes include French, history, geography, **civics**, math, science, and art.

After elementary school, French kids attend middle school until they are 15 years old. During these years, students decide what type of career they would like to pursue. From ages 16 to 18, students attend a *lycée*. This school prepares them for their future careers.

fun fact

The literacy rate is the percentage of people in a country who are able to read. The literacy rate in France is over 99 percent!

Did you know?

Many French children start school very young. Some start school when they are only 2 years old!

Did you know?

In 2008, more than 79 million people visited France, making it the world's top tourist destination.

Where People Work in France

manufacturing 24.3%

farming 3.8%

services 71.9%

More than half of the land in France is used for farming. Most farmers grow wheat, corn, barley, potatoes, grapes, peaches, or lemons. Some farmers raise cattle, hogs, sheep, and poultry. Fish are also an important food supply for the French.

Most French people have **service jobs** or work in factories or mines. French companies build cars, machinery, aircraft, and electronics. Many factories produce chemicals, clothing, or food products. Minerals mined in France include coal and iron ore. Tourism is the largest service industry in France. Many French people work in hotels, museums, and restaurants that serve travelers.

The French spend their free time watching TV, reading, and going to movies and plays. They also enjoy playing and watching sports. Soccer, rugby, and cycling are popular sports in France. Rugby is similar to American football, but players do not wear any padding.

France is famous for the Tour de France bike race. This three-week race covers more than 2,200 miles (3,500 kilometers) of Europe's countryside. Although the course changes every year, it always finishes in Paris.

fun fact

American Lance Armstrong won the Tour de France a record-breaking seven times in a row.

rugby

Food is an important part of French culture. The midday meal, the largest meal of the day, is traditionally eaten with the entire family. It begins with an appetizer, or *hors d'oeuvre*. This might consist of sausage, soup, raw vegetables, or liver paste called *pâté*. The main dish is called the *entrée*. It usually features seafood stew, fried steak, or roasted chicken or lamb. The *entrée* is often served with side dishes such as *ratatouille*, a mixed vegetable dish. Dessert is often a plate of fruit and cheese.

French food varies widely between regions. Cooks in the French Mediterranean use olive oil, **herbs**, and tomatoes in many dishes. Food in northwest France is made with butter and sour cream. Northeast France has strong German influences. Meals in this region often include sauerkraut. Seafood is commonly eaten along the French coasts.

fun fact

France boasts 500 different types of cheese. Local shops are constantly trying to create new kinds of cheese.

pâté

ratatouille

Mardi Gras

The French celebrate many holidays. The most famous French holiday is Mardi Gras. Many towns throw huge Mardi Gras carnivals that include floats and people in flashy costumes. The Feast of Kings, or *Fête des Rois*, is on January 6. The French celebrate this day with king cake. Most French people also celebrate Christmas.

The French enjoy a number of national holidays. On July 14, the French celebrate Bastille Day, which is Independence Day in France. Soldiers march in military parades to the beat of France's national anthem, *La Marseillaise*. At night, fireworks light up the sky while people dance in the streets.

Bastille Day

French Art and Architecture

The French are famous for their art and **architecture**. French artists developed **impressionism** in the 1800s. Rather than showing the details, impressionism gives the impression of a scene through unmixed paints and thick brushstrokes. Pierre-Auguste Renoir and Claude Monet were famous French impressionists.

Over the last several hundred years, the French have built many impressive buildings. *Notre Dame de Paris* is the most famous **cathedral** in France. One of the most well-known French landmarks is the Eiffel Tower, designed by Gustave Eiffel. Built between 1887 and 1889, it stands 1,063 feet (324 meters) tall. It was the tallest man-made structure in the world when it was completed. People from around the world come to see this symbolic monument and to learn more about French history and culture.

Eiffel Tower

fun fact
Almost 6 million people visit the Eiffel Tower every year.

Notre Dame de Paris

Fast Facts About France

France's Flag

France's flag is red, white, and blue. Red and blue are the traditional colors of France's capital, Paris. White was added to the flag for the rest of the country. The French Navy first used this flag design in 1790. The design was adopted by all of France in 1794.

Official Name: French Republic

Area: 248,429 square miles (643,427 square kilometers); France is the 42nd largest country in the world.

Capital City:	Paris
Important Cities:	Lyon, Marseille, Lille
Population:	64,057,792 (July 2010)
Official Language:	French
National Holiday:	Bastille Day (July 14)
Religions:	Christian (88%), Other (12%)
Major Industries:	manufacturing, mining, farming, fishing, services, tourism
Natural Resources:	coal, iron ore, bauxite, zinc, uranium, potash, feldspar, gypsum, wood, fish
Manufactured Products:	machinery, cars, aircraft, chemicals, food products, clothing
Farm Products:	wheat, sugar beets, potatoes, grapes, beef, dairy products
Unit of Money:	euro; the euro is divided into 100 cents.

Glossary

ancestors—relatives who lived long ago

architecture—the art or science of designing and constructing buildings

basin—an area of land surrounding a river

Basque people—a group of people who live in the western Pyrenees

cathedral—a large church

civics—studies related to being a good citizen of a country or community

gorges—deep, narrow valleys with steep, rocky sides

herbs—plants used in cooking; most herbs are used to add flavor to food.

impressionism—a style of painting that uses unmixed paints and thick brushstrokes; impressionism captures the impression of a scene rather than each small detail.

lowland—an area of land that is lower than the surrounding land

plateaus—areas of flat, raised land

service jobs—jobs that perform tasks for people or businesses

To Learn More

AT THE LIBRARY

Italia, Bob. *France*. Edina, Minn.: ABDO Publishing Company, 2001.

Nardo, Don. *France*. New York, N.Y.: Children's Press, 2008.

Sommers, Michael A. *France: A Primary Source Cultural Guide*. New York, N.Y.: PowerPlus Books, 2005.

ON THE WEB

Learning more about France is as easy as 1, 2, 3.

1. Go to www.factsurfer.com.

2. Enter "France" into the search box.

3. Click the "Surf" button and you will see a list of related Web sites.

With factsurfer.com, finding more information is just a click away.

Index